Penny Ante Feud 13

Between the shadow and the soul
(Pablo Neruda)

Penny Ante Feud 13: Between the shadow and the soul
is published by Shoe Music Press, Alpharetta, GA USA.
Its contents are protected by copyright law where applicable.

Cover image: *Wrestling—Sikeston, MO 1938*
in the Public Domain.

Penny Ante Feud has appeared in serial under ISSN:
2153-6422.

Email us at shoemusicpress@gmail.com and visit us
online at www.shoemusicpress.com

Salvatore Marici

Technical Knockout

Blue's right fist flies
at Red's face. Bash,
vessels break above his eye.
Padded mitten compresses
Red's temple.

Blue repeats the to and fro
with jackhammer speed.

Blood rushes
swells a skin sack over Red's eye
as his head hurls to a sharp halt
at the end of his extended neck.

Switchbacking brain
squeezes fluid out of ears,
shatters against the skull, scatters
and rattles under the crowd's cheer.

Ed Markowski

A Tribute

With thin blood tender tender calloused feet and a pacemaker propelling his ascension beyond the summit to refresh the poet tree planting new packets of strong steady words that were born bred and bathed in the salt of the Earth up and down a crazy star-pocked trail this sacrilegious saint and Saint Bernard who drained every drop of amber sanity from the bottomless barrel around his neck snap snap snapping photos of the decaying industrial guts of greed spilling lava hot from macro micro and Velcro America with an RG Dunn clenched firmly between his teeth flicking flies tagging trout and living wise in the soothing cool of an eternal Keweenaw stream carousing with his muse creating shaman songs gloriously drunk with the spirits of the B Brothers and our Grand Papa encased behind a warrior's sad eyes on the snow-shocked streets of a ghost-less ghost town after seventy-five years the white pine poet explores a new rock-topped superior shoreline that would kill a man half his age splashing his mad mind stew and painting his mind mad mural across a vast shifting snow-carved canvas dancing wolf wild through a shattered glass landscape in shoes that only he can fill.

Elena Botts

friday afternoon

bodies
splicing into commas
we are rapid
and we are
becoming incomplete
sentences
as the hot sun
makes my silhouette
dialectic (the swing
of your proportions are incalculable
geometries make my head
erratic
as ocean waves falling
sequentially, over and—)
your eyes so green and lovely that i hoped for
but faith was
something
contemplated
long after the screen
has been replaced
and the window shut.

Greg Moglia

Nest

At Sue's home here's the cardinal nest in the rhododendron
The babies just hatched, the mother on guard
Up above on the telephone line, the father scouting worms
I move in for a closer look and see how slight the cover

Sue says *Cats and raccoons the worry but the bush so slight*
Little chance for a good grip, anyway, the greatest danger from up above — hawks
I take it all in — the beauty of the Cardinals — the safety moves
The tension of it all — one easy breeze — the wrong leaf down

A clear view…route to the nest
Can't help think of us as seniors
Set up a host of protections, yet one time and one slip…
The next day Sue says *The babies gone…no cardinals…only the nest*

I'll give it to my granddaughter to take to school
I think yes, show the home
Show what in death
Goes on

Lurana Brown

Dispatched

What are their names,
those boys
in uniforms
in pictures
in museums

because they told each other
I'll never forget you
so someone must remember

forever words
through the silence, sounding
out of fields and stones
pounding hearts into dust
staining clothes with promises
and things to take back home are left

behind the velvet ropes
the messages unsent
still binding

Barbara Jay

Queen Cranberry

Julie stands on her tip toes in front of the big picture window.
She preens in the mirrored reflection.
Her smile takes flight.
Her heart beats fast.
Perfect she must be.

Her Mommy shuffles to the kitchen and starts the coffee.
She has knots in her stomach.
She busies herself with the laundry and ironing.
She lets her mind wander to the day she gave birth to her daughter.
She reaches for a tissue.
Then she winds her watch.

Across town, her Father throws his legs over the side of the bed.
Slowly he gets up, coughs, walks to the bathroom.
Just another day.
He dresses, skips breakfast and heads to the bar.
He hopes not to be the first one there.

Again, he has forgotten.

Slowly…deliberately…Julie prepares for her day with Daddy.
She wakes up early.
Bathes in fancy bubble bath.
Dresses in cranberry-red colors because he adores her in red.
Mommy carefully braids her hair and weaves in satiny ribbons.

White lacy ankle socks cushion her spit-shined black patent leather shoes.
Perfect she must be.

Her Mother wrinkles her forehead and sighs.
She looks through the movie listings…just in case.
Her heart aches at the thought.

Her Father is laughing with his friends oblivious to her anticipation.
He drinks beer and looks hopefully at the ladies.

Again, he has forgotten.

She asks Mommy what time it is.
She practices dancing to her Father's finger twirls in front of the window.
Quick.
She must twirl quickly in case she misses seeing him pull in front of the house.
She doesn't want to waste a moment.
Perfect she must be.

Mommy prepares lunch now.
They have to eat.
It's getting late.
She makes grilled cheese, Julie's favorite.
She looks for the chocolate milk in the refrigerator.
A favorite treat.
She worries. Please, not again…not again.

He listens to one last joke.
Slowly pulls away from the bar and absently wonders where he'll go next.

(Continued on page 8)

7

(Continued from page 7)

Again, he has forgotten.

It never dawned on Julie to sit.
She didn't want to get wrinkled or scuffed or smudged.
She stood tall.
She watched.
She was sure.
How much longer Mommy?

Mommy prays out loud: Soon, child, soon.

The football game finally lulls him to sleep.
The TV tray holds his half-eaten sandwich.
He never bothered to get undressed.

The sun was setting when Julie first moved from that window.
Slowly. Quietly.
She wilted toward her room.
Tears filled up her eyes.
She didn't understand.
She cried herself to sleep.

Mommy stood in the shower and hoped the water was loud enough.

Her Father woke with a start.
It was pitch black outside.
He thought he heard his name. Silly.
He grabbed a blanket and moved to the couch.
He drifted back to sleep.

Just another day.

Kurt Swalander

Letting Love Have a Killer Affair

Your heart once chained, now lost
in wild dreams & hopeless memories;
so many talkers guide the blindfolded

Our journey consists of quick conclusions seizing today
of past wants or constant Plan-B's;
never thinking far ahead

My heart pumps life to the releasing hand
fears the leash and loves the lady;
ran from an earthquake to get hit by a hurricane

My actions twined between love's ladies and love truly,
synopsis of you and I: youth, wisdom, counseling;
always were the greatest ears to which I spoke

Stacy Lynn Mar

Lover, I am Through With You

Reading your love letters
Is a lot like trying to concentrate
On one voice in an orchestration
Of background noise at the corner café.
Your longhand becomes
An alphabet of Egyptian hieroglyphic,
And again I've underestimated
The itch of my hands to touch the face
Of your story-teller's fiction.
For a moment I imagine I'm having
Coffee with Charles Bukowski at a country café
Somewhere outside the city limits
Of Santa Ana, California, if there is such a place.
He's smoking camel whites with his fritter cakes
And annotating the propensity of our
Preposterous, melodramatic arrangement.
No, he's really quite supportive in the
Down-home way he arranges his crepes,
A cup of coffee, and the late Sunday paper.
And I wonder what catastrophe awaits me
In the New York Times, whose uncle was killed,
Which sea the oil spoiled.
Negative dharma scratches the surface
Of my foresight like the heathens across
The room, grinding wooden chair legs into

Cheap marble flooring, as if it costs nothing
To refurbish a burning building, build a ruined life.
Wasn't it Aristotle who said happiness
Was the mere ebb and flow of life's dismantling
Moments…but he never survived the 20th century,
And somewhere in this vast atmosphere I'm sure
Rumi floats amongst the cloud dust
Of an exploding meteorite, waiting for the
World to burn its axis, that crooked brush stroke.
The words of your letters were written
To burn my eyes, to awaken the subconscious
Part of my after-affair with love, with you.
Each verb is strikingly similar to a sucker-punch,
Did you think I would not decipher the code
You wrote between those college-ruled lines?
Stacy is a pretty girl, Stacy is a fool.
Tomorrow I will be done with 3am
High heel logic, with stone slabs tuning me out,
I will be done with yesterday's rune work.
At least then you will love me, when it's too late.
"Ciao," says the clock in the watchtower,
The stars blink in agreement, the witches hang the moon.

David Huntley

Faded Vision

Violently singing at the chalk dust Moon
Coward blood ringing through cobbled carpet
Faded knives in the blur of blustered sleet
Ten Marlboro Lights and a kissed light neon tendril
Tangled tweed flower
Weeds and thorns
Grass veiled thorns smoke filled septum
Tearing nostrils with bloodied nails
One smart hit then down
Recovery position
Firefly Hymns insinuating the night sky
Clambering over the bridge
Chips thrown over into murky water
Let the dogs loose when I stab and let
Them tear out the heart
Burn out into the depths
Only to be brought back to the surface
By Fishing lines hung on the sandy hook
Piercing through the testament navy darkness
Phlegm coughed laughter croaking at
Midnight Stars.

Georg Kickinger

Beyond The Jagged Coastline

I'll cut out god's eyes
to make him feel that
which he only knows about
in his office of wisdom.

You, naked and dripping wet
watch the kelp, it bobs up and down
in this pleasure galaxy
falling, adrift on our barge
grind my ashes to the bone.

Already beneath doric columns
blood-leathered boots and
nailed to the streets, I saw you
hold the cards, spread them
anew with your limbs
in daphne-scented fields.

Your reed hunger I uncoil
in your wild rose dirt marshes
I rise, my face against the moon
hung to the rails, fuck me innocent.

(Continued on page 14)

13

(Continued from page 13)

Gladly, I free-dive
your dark cotton well water
stripped completely bare
shred me to pieces
for me to abandon
what is only food for the blind
ferryman's eyes reflecting
round tables squared
meals that stuff the throat
with dowry stones.

What else can I hurtle against
the stingray-shot but make you roar
with satisfaction and find the spots
that send you burst into giggles
that leave me smiling still
when by the roadside I stand
and wave and watch you
drive away.

Alan Catlin

Sideshow Extras

On all those carnival lit nights,
fish smoked and dirt flavored,
rancorous with sick drunk
revelers stumbling to the tents.
Hand painted sign outside
ragged edge flaps says,
"Little Poison"; not quite
fortunes told, cards picked
from stacked decks, every face
turned up, a fool or a knave,
a hanged man or a wronged woman,
jagged paths and precipitous
cliffs. A journey to the east
is told in tattoos on her body,
impressions amplified by boa
constrictor arm wraps,
slow turning skin hypnotic
as spells cast for an unnamed
price, for small death promises
in each lethally cast eye.
Emanating smoke of many dreams
for all the sideshow extras bound for
undisclosed destinations,
in unknown places. Once inside,
there is no turning back.

Sarah Gawricki

the gauntlet

(click clack)
im so lucky i found this

    and what's that?
(back back)
a way to stretch a grave into a gauntlet
    pause
(enter.)

<u>Tina Garvin</u>

No. 27

To make a mountain

made of sand breaks many rakes

Before the sunrise

John McCleod

Ainissesthai
(Greek, to speak in riddles)

… dangling, as a puppet on strings;
Twisting … , in a gale of silence;
Suspended, … between light and dark,
Between the … secret and public,
Between the masses … and the void;
Disconnected, incorporeal …;
Alienated, dissociated; …
There is no escape, no … nepenthe,
No recourse, savior, or rescue ….
Our course is unavoidable, …
Our future shared, entwined, … alike.
Appeased, I am waiting … for you.

Patrick Longe

the handle heavy

an existential
 jack-in-the-box
the vernacular
 smacks the libido

words, the bandits
 next door
 next table
 next seat

the crux, leaves
 gray
 green
 yellow

or just pale, face
 to own thoughts
of trigger hold

and so spent, to
 the innocuous

(Continued on page 20)

19

(Continued from page 19)

figure of speech
        drips so sweet
        tastes so relevant

sucked, to the stop
 of the existential
jack-in-the-box

Alex Nevin

Rising Above

I've been trying hard
to rise above
it but
here I am
slow and sedate
caught up in a mode
of thinking
that can't be undone
when you are around
I am all lit up
when you're gone I feel like
an empty cup
fuck.
When I think
of your memory
I sleep on hardwood floors
in daylight
stay up all night
eat stolen cheesecake
and watch stars in transit.

Ivan de Monbrison

La chute

l'eau frotte
contre
ce flanc vulgaire
la nuit pénètre par la peau
aveugle
tu te guides
lentement
à l'aide de la rambarde
qui dénonce
la chute
d'une pente peu fiable qui en découle
ainsi ces falaises habitées par des oiseaux de
proies
ne sont-elles vivables
que pour les morts
ou bien pour
leurs sosies de lumière

The falling

the water rubbing
against
this vulgar flank
the night enters through the skin
blind
you guide yourself
slowly
using the railing
which denounces
the falling
of an unreliable slope effusing from it
so these cliffs inhabited by birds of prey
aren't livable
but by the dead
or by
their luminous lookalikes

Greendream

Trees

The trees
They have spoken
Leaves fall like tears
Children build houses in your branches
A hideout for the bank robber
Or maybe the forgotten soldier
You're a daydreamer's dream
A place to telescope the sky
Limbs have been cut
Yet you are still alive
Sap bleeding wounds will heal
The ladder of nails
I crucified you with
The
Roots
Are
Deep
As
The
Soul

Andrew Weston

The Future is Crayon

That's me.
The one sat in the corner, writing on your wall and eating crayons.
Yeah,
Now you know why my language is so colorful,
Asshole!
You smother my creativity in the straightjacket of brain-vomit,
Spewed from the gaping holes of the masses,
And have the gall to imagine
That I'd put on your rose-tinted spectacles,
And give you a High-Five?

I'll give you five alright.
In fact, they come in pairs called *Left* and *Right*.
Here, enjoy them both,
Bam! Bam!
You look so much better without your teeth,
Fucker!

Did you honestly think
You could stamp my passport to the land of the bland,
And sneak my bleached-out mind through customs?
"Have you anything to declare, Sir,"
Hell yes!
I'm stuck on six o'clock,

(Continued on page 26)

25

(Continued from page 25)

And I'm already late for my own tea party.
But what do you care?

Medicated, I'm about as spontaneous as a cliff and
as subtle as a nail-gun.
So, do me a favor,
Get down off my camel,
Stuff your hand down your throat,
Grab your nuts, and pull hard!
Please, turn yourself inside out,
I could do with a laugh.
Better still,
Give me a blunt knife and I'll cut them off for you.

Michael Estabrook

Heat Wave

When you get to be my age
95 degrees is dangerous
stay indoors
in front of the fan
hydrate hydrate hydrate

Time for me to get up
on the ladder shirtless at mid-day
finish painting the gutter and overhang
I enjoy taunting the gods
they've been taunting me
for 65 years already
the sons of bitches!

John Grey

Tales of the Drowning Man

First I thrash about crazily,
then I just let my body sink.
I am in a panic
but a resignation overtakes it
I gasp snatches of air,
breathe water easily.
Above is rescue,
below is death,
and this last is
where I am headed.
I hit bottom
and I close my eyes.
It is like I am sleeping.
In fact, I am sleeping.
But I don't dream.
I just get ideas.

Sunny Cook

The Sand Castle Gang

Girls with sun streaked hair and Hawaiian print bikinis
worked the sand with their trowels.
Guys in batik print surfer pants carried water from
the shoreline.
The cool kids from Avocet High School carried out their
plans for another winning sand castle.   The trick was to
get as close to the water's edge without having the
structure crumble by a rogue wave.
The turrets were high and very detailed. The in crowd would
win again.   But...nothing is certain.
A lone wave had a different idea and dragged the masterpiece
out to sea.   How could this happen on such a calm day?
The architects were humbled and hung their heads. They all
thought of Scott, the slightly autistic kid from the resource room.
He asked repeatedly to join the group, because he claimed to
have great insight in building castles.   Dusty was the first to say
what they were all thinking, "Let's invite Scott for the end of
summer contest."

Richard King Perkins II

Intrinsecus

An intimation, an intonation,
a being never met and always known
gentle frictions and blessed grandeur
slippery voices purr past dark ennui
offering acute angles in fait accompli.
Espied from rhythmic candlesticks
envy our insensibility— we cling like dust
pressed and akimbo greater particles
breathing but unknown.
Heated ablution given to spasm
a lost kiss, worlds confined in simple flesh.
Your eyes, a language in reverse,
undoing me completely
my words— my fingers—
keys that ever open.
Is it love my love, in fluid whisper—

snap

and it is gone.

Philip Kobylarz

New Englandy

At the gate, bottles with cut lips. Crypts of grass cuttings. Moth wings. Stationary
weather front. Still
a front. At the gate, a trail worn thick. Strands of birch. Playing cards wet
and mangled in
alleys, no jokers. At the gate, a gate. Handles, pulled. Insouciant. Towards
a line of people bent
on waiting. At the gate, a passage to. Through the gate: changeling of fences.

Cathy Bryant

Force

I have seen blossoms come and go
and come and go again in many Springs;
I have seen the murmuration of starlings dapple
the garden with their dance,
and bats whirring at dusk, night-swallows
out to dine on a fine tapas of insects;
I have smelt fragrant smoke that flowed
through flower-heavy summer air
and I sipped cold champagne or gulped it
and I sang. I sang.

Air, the air, I have tasted the air
of a Welsh mountain and flown above
the very clouds in an outlandish
metal creature. I have read thousands
of books and, through them, travelled
in every country, city and planet
that ever was or was not, and into the minds
of the women and men and aye, children
("Mr. Saltena was an elderly gentleman of forty two")
who wrote them.

I have known the blank numbness of utter despair
after the motors of sobbing have broken down,
and the silence that follows when the pillow grows
cold with the wet of all the tears. I have known love,

ah love! I have passioned to the stars and never
come back. I have kept my seat on a bolting horse,
and fallen off a pony.

I have felt pain now for twenty five years,
and it never goes away.
Only the living feel pain.
I have sculpted snow, snow that changes
the eyes and ears of the world,
making alien places for us.
I have seen the sea frozen.
I have felt hope, and laughed at things
other than myself. I have made
an audience scream with laughter,
eyes pleasure-bright.

I've known strange and wonderful inventions:
bicycles, contraception, microwaves,
roller skates, antibiotics, socks;
I have pressed a button and heard
an orchestra play a symphony.
I have pressed a button and stopped
that orchestra mid-movement.
I have built a fire and put one out.
I have touched gold, velvet, living fur,
diamonds, grass, glass, hot sand,
seawater, concrete, steel, thorns,
roses, lettuce, custard, strangers,

(Continued on page 34)

(Continued from page 33)

presents, long wind-rippled hair.
I have sent and received messages
to and from all the places of the world.

And this is only the millionth part
of the millionth part of my luck and joy.

Harold Whit Williams

Neon Yellow Pillow Fight
Leaving Narita Airport, 1996

Konichiwa, dear driver, please pull over.
I can't hold it any longer. Too much Asahi.
I would love to read and comprehend

Your road signs. This one might say –
The Sky Here Is A Facsimile Of Itself
That No One Bothers To Looks At.

That one over there might say – Please
Maybe Rock And Roll Goodbye Now.
I'm guessing your sky today is gunmetal grey

Because this cold weather feels like some
Slow cinema bullet. I would love to stand here
Waxing poetic about starling flocks overhead,

How they shapeshift their murmurations into
The likeness of Mount Fuji, or a stubby penis,
Or Emperor Hirohito's eyeglasses. I would love

To keep standing here, relieving my bladder
On your entire country, nourishing the fields
For that coming rice crop. I would love

(Continued on page 36)

(Continued from page 35)

To read a road sign that said — Everything
Will Be A-OK. I would love to, just once,
Someday see someone else's original sky.

Laura Taylor

I-Museum

Come and see the I-Museum.

No curtains, no blinds, no nets. Blinding sometimes.

The exhibits change day to day. Who seeks comfort in the linear?

The building disappears if you enter it in anger. The floors withdraw, the walls collapse. You can only visit if you are peaceful and calm. The entrance only opens if your eyes are smiling.

There is no Authority, it's self-policing. Less trouble that way. More responsibility.

If you don't maintain a peaceful equilibrium, the building disappears around you.

Although sometimes, if you get a rage on inside, the ceilings ignite. Depends on the rage.

In the foyer, there's a framed photo of a small girl smiling with her mouth. The photo is black and white. The dress is pink and hated.

The first room has cartoon-like cakes, bursting out the tops of their wrappers. Sumptuous, exciting, begging to be eaten.

(Continued on page 38)

37

(Continued from page 37)

You can't, of course. If you try, the building disappears around you. The musical room contains a gnawed wooden recorder. It smells of pre-pubescent spit, sweaty fingers, and school.

To open the door of the musical room, take a deep breath and hold it. To exit, do this in reverse.

Don't touch the handle — the door will slam onto your fingers. You will breathe in. Entropy will ensue.

In the café there's a radiogram, locked within a nicotine-stained-glass case. No money required. The turntable revolves around levels of memory. 78s will play if opening bars of songs can be sung.

If you sing too loudly, the shellac scratches and the glass case fills with smoke.

The reading room contains 5 books, which have been read approximately 50 times each. The spines are broken. If you pick them up, pages fall out, and the building disappears around you. Leave the books alone, get your own.

There's a flat-chested Cindy doll in that room over there, with shorn hair and home-made clothes. A stolen Action Man keeps Cindy company, and they mostly fight or fuck.

In the cellar there's a well of tears, soon to boil and dry. And all the implements you'd ever need to raise weals on a small girl. There are curtains down there, that are permanently closed, so people can't see in.

Jennifer Currier

Three Little Words That Say It All

My cheeks as red
As my ass
After you were through

Blushing bride
But not yours
Why not yours

Nothing as amazing
As the feel of you
On me inside me

Gentle lips
Gripping hands
Thrusting hips

Nothing as sweet
As those three little words
Burned into my soul

Softly brutal
On all accounts
Is that your purpose

Rip me apart
Again
Then fix it

Each time better
Yet
Ending worse

I crave
I want
I need

Nothing like you
No one like you
No love like yours

Colin James

Safe Murder

The cloud hovered perpetually
over the still lake.
At this exact moment
on the opposite shore,
survivalists are launching a boat.
Provocateurs of light-starved water,
they haunt the edges
of my tea cup saucer.
This is like catching a break,
we are usually well into
the liturgy by now.

J. J. Steinfeld

A Precise Calculus of Near Poetic Death

At a newly renovated bar
windowless as perfected darkness
midtown fading midafternoon
the former poet (definition his)
like a huge honourable mention
from a befuddled judge
claims he has no more
than five beers a day
(but no less, mind you)
a precise calculus
of near poetic death
then utters, a bit of foam
at the corner of his mouth,
"Mourning for the lost morning,"
and laughs, says today he will
shatter the calculus
if I buy him a sixth beer
I say yes, compassion or pity
(difficult to diagnose)
bring up the play title
Mourning Becomes Electra
he guesses Eugene O'Neill
(surprise-quiz impressive)
and I leave before

(Continued on page 44)

43

(Continued from page 43)

the former poet finishes his beer
or comes up with another line
of broken poetry.

Ed Coletti

Dead Career

He clutches for its puffy corpse
bobbing below/above surface
rolling with it astride it

rodeo rider rolling sea
choked with briny gulps
gasps for air any air

rises to lookout
scans Pacific
largest mass

finds no sail no ship
clutches for its bloated corpse again
riding it for all he's worth.

Peter Victor

The Snow Cave

The air was crystal clear
And cold
The sky
A deep blue

And very beautiful
The snow was deep
And the clearing surrounded
By ancient hardwood

The snow of the clearing was trampled everywhere
And stained
A deep red
The body lay on the other side of the clearing

Massive, motionless and dead
He sat and stared
On his butt in the snow
Aware of his own injuries

And his life
Seeping into the white snow
As he stared
But he could not look away

The encounter had been a long time in coming
It was not if, but when and where
And now it was over
It ended as it had to…with an end

He knew
Loss
Something he had lived with forever
Was finally dead

He shook his head and came out of his trance
He knew
He did not have much time
He propped himself up with the broken ski

And slowly, painfully, turned around
His eyes rested on the small knoll
He began crawling, dragging the broken ski
Through the trampled, blood stained snow

Reaching the base of the knoll
Using the broken ski
He began to dig
A grave or a bed – he did not know

He did not have much room to move
Dirt, small rocks and melted snow
Were in his face, mouth and neck
He held his gloves in his bare hand and ran them
over his face

He struggled to remove his coat
Then rolled on top
Sweat covered his face
His hands gently probed his body, then lay still

(Continued on page 48)

(Continued from page 47)

His vision began to blur
He slowly closed his eyes
And was drifting
Shadowy known figures began to emerge

Then he was gone

New to Penny Ante Feud? You'll want to catch up on our back issues:

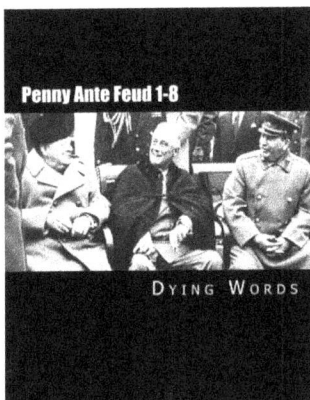

Penny Ante Feud 1-8 — DYING WORDS

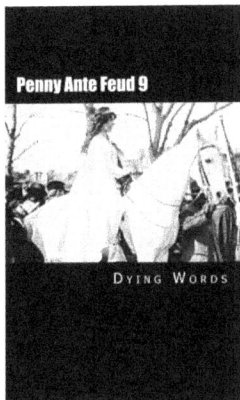

Penny Ante Feud 9 — DYING WORDS

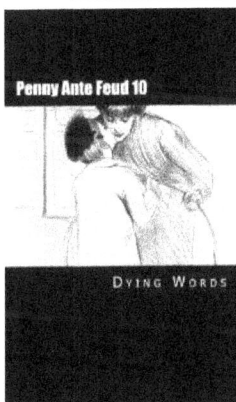

Penny Ante Feud 10 — DYING WORDS

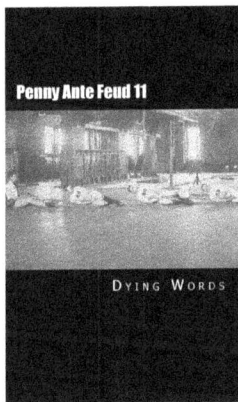

Penny Ante Feud 11 — DYING WORDS

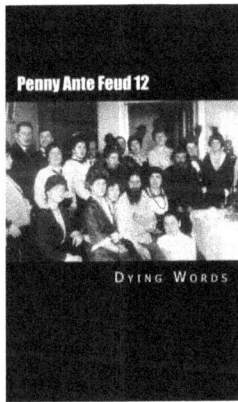

Penny Ante Feud 12 — DYING WORDS

Please check our website www.shoemusicpress.com for current pricing (special bulk discount and author pricing available).

www.ingramcontent.com/pod-product-compliance
Lightning Source LLC
Chambersburg PA
CBHW060624030426
42337CB00018B/3184